Reclaiming The Joy & Honor of Motherhood:

Exposing the Truth About Postpartum Depression

Dr. Latina Campbell

Print ISBN: **978-1-966491-187**

eBook ISBN: **978-1-966491-194**

Printed in the United States of America

Story Corner Publishing & Consulting, Inc.

Chesapeake, VA 23321

Storycornerpublishing@yahoo.com

www.StoryCornerPublishing.com

Dedication

I dedicate this book to all the mothers fighting for joy, peace, a healthy mind, to live & not die, and fighting to raise their children God's way. I see you and you are doing a fantastic job! I am proud of you, and I am sending love and prayers your way. Life gets hard sometimes, but that is normal. It is ok to take a break, so your mind and body reset itself. Self-care and Spirit-care are very important. Therefore, put it on your calendar and become intentional concerning yourself.

Showing up as your best self will benefit you and your family.

Table of Contents

Introduction

Reclaiming the Truth About Motherhood

Motherhood is one of the most sacred and powerful callings God has given to women. Through you, life enters the world, fulfilling His command to "be fruitful and multiply" (Genesis 1:28). Yet today, this divine role has been clouded by fear, doubt, and discouragement. One of the most subtle yet damaging ways this has happened is through the rise and labeling of what's commonly known as "postpartum depression."

Yes, the emotional and physical challenges women face after childbirth are real—and they matter. But labeling these struggles as a disorder has created a culture of fear around motherhood. You've likely heard it: that having children leads to mental instability, emotional despair, or a complete loss of identity. These messages aren't just misleading—they're designed to make you question your God-given ability to nurture and lead a family.

But this fear is not just cultural—it's spiritual. In Genesis 3:15, God declared that Satan would always be at war with the seed of the woman. That war is still raging. From abortion to the subtle messages that make motherhood feel unbearable, the enemy's goal is clear: to silence the womb, discourage women, and destroy the next generation.

Why? Because Satan knows the power of a godly mother. When you raise children in the fear of the Lord, you're planting seeds that can change generations, disrupt darkness, and advance the kingdom of God.

The idea of "postpartum depression" has become one of the enemy's strategies. It amplifies fear, downplays faith, and discourages women from stepping confidently into their role as life-givers. Meanwhile, governments and global institutions often promote fear-based narratives to suppress birth rates, push population control, and undermine the value of family—all while claiming to support women.

Yet when we look at other parts of the world, we see a different story. Many cultures don't experience postpartum depression the way it's understood in the West. Why? Because they prioritize biblical principles like community, support, and shared responsibility. These values provide the emotional, spiritual, and practical support new mothers need—values that have been eroded in individualistic societies.

This book aims to uncover the truth. It exposes the spiritual warfare behind modern narratives about motherhood. It challenges the fear-based mindset and replaces it with biblical truth, hope, and encouragement.

Together, we'll explore:

- How the enemy attacks mothers through fear, lies, and isolation.
- The societal and political agendas that devalue motherhood and limit family growth.
- The true sources of a mother's emotional struggle—often rooted in unmet needs, not childbirth itself.
- How you can reclaim your joy, purpose, and identity in Christ to thrive as a mother and raise children who honor God.

Motherhood is not a burden—it's a blessing. The struggles you face are not signs of failure. They are invitations to grow deeper in faith, to become more resilient, and to lean into God's strength. You were never meant to walk this journey alone, and you are more equipped than you realize.

This is your call to rise. If you've ever doubted your ability to mother well, feared the weight of motherhood, or struggled to reconcile your challenges with the joy you longed for—this message is for you.

It's time to silence the lies.

Reclaim the truth.

And walk boldly into the divine calling of motherhood.

My Testimony

I remember it like it was yesterday.

I had just gotten married and was pregnant with baby number four. This was supposed to be one of the happiest moments of my life. But instead of joy, we were facing homelessness. Neither my husband nor I had a job. We had no family to lean on, no village to support us, and I felt abandoned—even by God.

What I didn't know at the time was that we were in the wilderness, being prepared for transition. God wasn't punishing us— He was positioning us.

But in that moment, it didn't feel that way. People laughed at us. Talked about us. Treated us with cruelty instead of compassion. I sank into depression, overwhelmed by the weight of it all. It felt like the longest, hardest season of my life.

My marriage began to suffer. My husband's family never accepted me and constantly interfered, trying to control him and divide our home. They became a wedge between us, but what God put together, no man could tear apart. That's why He had to separate us from everyone coming against the covenant He created.

One Sunday, I didn't even want to go to church. I was still pregnant and emotionally exhausted. The Apostle approached me and asked, "Are you suffering from postpartum depression?" I was stunned. Offended, even. I wasn't postpartum—I was still carrying my child! And not once had she asked what I was going through.

It was in that moment I realized how casually and carelessly people throw that term around. I had expected more from her, especially as a mother of eight who had endured 13 evictions and seasons of homelessness herself. Instead, she parroted what the world says—what doctors and media are trained to promote.

I couldn't believe it. How had we been so deceived?

The trials I faced weren't because I was pregnant. They weren't caused by my baby. They were the result of life circumstances, poor decisions, spiritual warfare, and emotional pain. My husband should have turned to God for guidance instead of the voices tearing us apart. I should've stood firmer in my faith. But none of it was because of the child growing inside me.

I wasn't depressed because I had a baby—I was depressed because I didn't understand what God was doing. I didn't know why He united us in marriage, gave us children, and then allowed such intense pain. Sleeping in a car, hearing our babies cry out of fear and hunger—it felt unbearable. I wondered if I had failed completely, not just as a mother, but as a woman. I even asked God to take me because I couldn't see a way out.

But now I see clearly: what the world calls postpartum depression is often a demonic attack against our minds and our callings. It's not just a chemical imbalance or a diagnosis—it's a spiritual weapon formed to make us question our worth, our purpose, and God's promise.

Motherhood is a sacred ministry. And yes, it's hard. But what we go through isn't proof that we're failing—it's proof that the enemy is terrified of the power we carry.

We have work to do. Kingdom work. Work that only we as mothers can fulfill.

Don't accept the labels. Don't accept the lies. You are not broken. You are not crazy. You are chosen, and God is with you— even in the wilderness.

Chapter 1:

The Biblical Perspective on Motherhood and the Seed of Women

Let's be clear from the start: your motherhood is not a coincidence. It's not a fallback plan or something you "just ended up doing." It's a divine assignment, handcrafted by God Himself. Before the world told you what you should or shouldn't do with your body, your time, or your dreams—God had already spoken over you: "Be fruitful and multiply, fill the earth and subdue it." (Genesis 1:28)

That command wasn't simply about having babies—it was about shaping nations, birthing legacy, and partnering with heaven to populate the earth with purpose.

But here's the truth the enemy doesn't want you to remember: your womb is powerful. And because of that, it's been under attack since the beginning.

The Battle You Didn't Ask For—But Were Born to Win

In Genesis 3:15, God declared war on Satan. He said to the serpent:

"I will put enmity between you and the woman, and between your offspring and hers; he will crush your head, and you will strike his heel."

That moment wasn't just a punishment for the serpent. It was a prophetic declaration: your children carry purpose. Your seed is dangerous to darkness. And because of that, the enemy has targeted mothers—and their children—ever since.

Every time you nurture, teach, or even carry a child, you're waging war against hell itself. Your love, your prayers, your protection—it all counts in the spiritual realm.

Recognizing Satan's Attacks on Motherhood

Mama, look around. The enemy's fingerprints are all over history:

- Pharaoh ordered Hebrew baby boys to be killed.
- Herod tried to wipe out infants in his quest to destroy Jesus.
- Today, abortion is presented as a "right" rather than the spiritual crisis it is.
- Postpartum depression, isolation, and mom guilt are quietly silencing strong women like you every day.

These are not just natural challenges. They are spiritual strategies. The enemy knows that if he can discourage you from mothering boldly, he can delay the rise of future warriors.

Your Children Are Not a Burden—They're Arrows

God's Word never calls children a hassle or inconvenience. Instead, He calls them a reward.

"Children are a heritage from the Lord, offspring a reward from him… Like arrows in the hands of a warrior…" (Psalm 127:3-5)

That means you are a warrior, and every child you raise is a weapon against the enemy's camp. Every bedtime prayer, every correction, every moment of nurturing—you are sharpening arrows for God's kingdom.

So, when culture tells you:

- *"Wait to have children."*
- *"They'll ruin your career."*
- *"You don't need a man."*
- *"Motherhood is a trap."*

Remember who's really talking. That voice isn't God's. It's the same one that spoke in Eden, sowing doubt and division.

The Lie That Motherhood Holds You Back

No, motherhood doesn't limit you—it unlocks you. It awakens strength you didn't know you had, love you didn't know existed, and purpose deeper than titles or paychecks. While there's nothing wrong with ambition or success, they were never meant to replace the joy and impact of raising godly children.

You're not "just a mom." You're a legacy builder. A spiritual warrior. A kingdom nurturer.

And the world needs more of you.

Look to the Mothers in the Bible

When you're feeling unsure, overwhelmed, or unseen— remember the women God used:

Hannah refused to give up in her barrenness. She prayed—and God gave her Samuel, a prophet to a nation.

Jochebed hid her baby in a basket to save his life. That baby became Moses, Israel's deliverer.

Mary said "yes" to the impossible—and gave birth to the Savior of the world.

None of these women had perfect conditions. But they had faith. And that faith changed everything.

So, mama, it's not about being perfect—it's about being willing. Willing to trust God with your children. Willing to fight in prayer. Willing to see your motherhood the way He sees it.

When Motherhood Feels Heavy—God Strengthens You

There will be days when it's all too much. When sleep is scarce, and doubts are loud. But even then, God is with you.

Let His Word carry you:

- "He gives strength to the weary…" (Isaiah 40:29)
- "I can do all things through Christ…" (Philippians 4:13)
- "God is our refuge and strength…" (Psalm 46:1)

You're not raising your child alone. The same God who gave you this child will equip you to raise them well.

Reclaiming the Truth About Motherhood

Let's change the narrative, together. Let's stop echoing the world and start declaring what heaven says:

- Motherhood is not a curse—it's a calling.
- Children are not a setback—they're a setup for legacy.
- You are not less because you're a mom—you're more than enough in Christ.

Your Call to Rise Up

This is your time to take your rightful place—not just as a caretaker, but as a kingdom influencer. Every lullaby, every diaper change, every meal prepared—it all matters in God's eyes. You are participating in a holy work.

Therefore, let's rise up together, mama:

- Reject the lie that motherhood is a burden.
- Receive the truth that your children are blessings.
- Raise them intentionally, knowing they carry heaven's DNA.
- Encourage other mothers to walk boldly in their callings.

The enemy fears mothers who understand their worth. He fears homes filled with God's presence. And he trembles at generations raised in faith.

Here's the question: Will you rise up and reclaim your role?

Not just for yourself.

Not just for your children.

But for the generations yet to come.

Because when mothers rise, kingdoms advance.

And Mama—you were born for this.

Chapter 2:

Reclaiming Your Mind—Breaking Free from the PPD Label

Let's talk plainly. The world has given a name to what you're feeling: "postpartum depression." And while some parts of that label might describe your emotions, I want to dig deeper than that surface-level diagnosis. I want to speak to the part of you that's questioning if you're broken... if you're failing... if something is wrong with you because joy didn't flood in the moment your baby arrived.

Hear me clearly: you are not broken—you are becoming. This transition is holy. And holy things often come with pain, stretching, and surrender.

Yes, you're tired. Yes, your hormones are shifting. Yes, your body feels foreign and your mind overwhelmed. But before we call it a disorder, let's call it what it is: transformation.

Postpartum depression has become a catch-all phrase used to describe what many mothers go through after childbirth. But mama, what if this isn't depression as the world sees it? What if it's spiritual resistance? What if what you're feeling is part of a divine process—and the enemy is trying to label it so you won't fight back?

Let's stop accepting fear as normal. Let's stop letting society tell us that this journey is doomed from the start.

The Truth the World Won't Tell You

Modern culture has turned motherhood into a clinical experience. The minute you express sadness or fatigue, you're handed a label and a prescription. But mama, no one stops to ask if what you're feeling is a call to go deeper with God, or if maybe—just maybe—you're carrying more than your baby. You're carrying generational healing. Purpose. A legacy.

And that kind of weight? It's not easy. But it's not depression—it's spiritual birth.

You're Not Sick—You're Shifting

This is not about denying that some women truly suffer and need professional support. But it's also not about ignoring the spiritual roots of the struggle. Satan wants to hijack your mind in this vulnerable time. He whispers that you're weak, that you're alone, that your baby deserves someone better.

But God says otherwise.

You are not less than—you are chosen.

You are not incapable—you are equipped.

You are not falling apart—you are being rebuilt.

How Culture Feeds the Fear

From the moment you announced your pregnancy, you were likely warned more than encouraged. "Sleep now while you can." "You'll never have time for yourself again." "Watch out for postpartum depression."

It was fear from the beginning. But fear is not from God.

Culture has created a postpartum narrative full of dread. And you, mama, are living out a story God wrote with joy, strength, and grace. The disconnect between His truth and the world's version is enough to make anyone feel disoriented.

Let's Talk About Your Thoughts

Your thoughts are powerful. They are seeds. What you water will grow. If you repeat the lies—"I'm failing," "I can't do this," "I'm not enough"—you'll start to believe them. But if you begin to speak life—"God is with me," "I am being strengthened," "I was made for this"—you'll shift the entire atmosphere of your home.

Scripture says, "Be transformed by the renewing of your mind" (Romans 12:2). That transformation starts with what you think and say about yourself.

Here's what I want you to declare:

- "This season is stretching me, not destroying me."
- "I am not my emotions—I am God's daughter."
- "God chose me to mother this child. He will sustain me."

When It Feels Too Heavy

I know there are days when the tears won't stop, when you can't hear God clearly, and you feel like you're drowning in diapers, dishes, and doubt. That doesn't make you faithless. It makes you human.

Even Jesus withdrew to rest.

Even David cried out in anguish.

Even Elijah begged for death under a tree.

God never turned them away. And He won't turn you away either.

So, lean into Him. Cry if you must. But don't stop showing up for your healing. Postpartum isn't a pit you're stuck in—it's a tunnel you're walking through. And God's light is up ahead.

Practical Steps to Guard Your Mind

1. Speak life daily. Don't let one lie go unchallenged. Replace every negative thought with Scripture.
2. Rest without guilt. Sleep is not a luxury—it's a weapon.
3. Feed your spirit. Read the Word, even if it's just one verse a day. Let God's truth saturate your soul.
4. Surround yourself with faith-filled women. Isolation is the enemy's playground. Find your people.
5. Don't be afraid to get help. Faith and professional support are not enemies—they can work together.

What No One Tells You

You were never meant to do this alone. In many cultures, mothers are surrounded by community, care, and prayer. But in our Western society, women are told to "bounce back" before they even heal. That's not God's way.

-God's way is rest.

-God's way is renewal.

-God's way is restoration.

Mama, Reframe This Season

Stop calling it depression.

Start calling it a transition.

Start calling it a spiritual awakening.

Start calling it the birth of your next level.

This is not your end. This is your emergence.

God is not disappointed in you—He's developing you.

You are not losing your identity—you are finding a deeper version of it.

You are not broken—you are becoming whole.

So breathe, beloved. Rest in His presence. Trust the process. You are walking through the fire, but you won't be burned. You're just being refined.

And when you come out of this, you won't even look like what you've been through.

Chapter 3:

Unveiling the U.S. Government's Role in Suppressing Birth Rates

Have you ever wondered why you sometimes feel like you're swimming against the current just to live out your God-given role? You know in your spirit that motherhood is a sacred calling, yet society often makes you feel like it's a burden, an inconvenience—even a mistake. That's not just coincidence. What you're feeling is real. There are spiritual forces at work, yes—but there are also powerful, intentional political agendas working behind the scenes.

Let's talk about that.

While your personal struggles are intimate and emotional, they don't exist in a vacuum. You're living in a culture shaped by decades of policies, programs, and propaganda designed to suppress birth rates and devalue motherhood. And many of those ideas started right here in the United States.

The Myth They've Sold You

You've likely heard it: "The world is overpopulated." It's repeated so often that it almost feels like truth. But this idea is based on flawed thinking—fears that there won't be enough food, clean water, or space for everyone. Scripture tells a different story. In Genesis 1:29–30, God provided for His creation abundantly. What we often call "shortage" is usually just mismanagement, greed, or unjust systems—not lack.

Behind the scenes, the U.S. government has funded global programs that push birth control, sterilization, and abortion—not simply as options, but as solutions. And guess who these programs target most? Women who look like you. Women raising children in poor, minority, or developing communities. The message is subtle, but clear: You shouldn't have more children.

How Policies Have Shaped Your Struggle

You're not imagining the financial pressures, the lack of support, or the workplace resistance. These things didn't appear out of nowhere—they were designed.

- Economic Strain: The cost of raising children in the U.S. has skyrocketed. Healthcare, childcare, education—everything feels like it's working against you. And there's little to no real support for mothers who want to stay home or raise larger families.
- Workplace Pressures: Maternity leave is often too short. Returning to work feels like choosing between providing for

your child and being present in their life. Your devotion gets labeled as weakness or lack of ambition.

- Abortion Advocacy Masquerading as Empowerment: The narrative says, "You're in control of your body." But really, it's about controlling birth rates. And often, that "empowerment" doesn't come with resources for keeping your child—only for ending the pregnancy.

- Fear-Based Messaging: From news reports to school textbooks, the world paints motherhood as exhausting, financially irresponsible, and emotionally draining. Rarely do you hear the joys, the eternal impact, or the spiritual strength it builds.

These aren't just cultural opinions. They are part of a long-term political agenda that quietly whispers, Don't have too many. Don't depend on anyone. Don't expect help. Don't choose motherhood.

You Are Not the Problem—You Are the Solution

When governments prioritize productivity over people, and convenience over life, they begin to devalue the very foundation of society: the family. You may have noticed how fathers are often removed from the conversation altogether—how single motherhood is normalized, but not truly supported. This, too, is strategic.

You weren't meant to mother in isolation. God designed families to be interdependent, not independent. And yet, culture celebrates self-sufficiency while leaving you to carry the emotional, physical, and financial weight of raising a child—alone.

But hear this: Your decision to have a child is an act of courage. Your commitment to raising them in faith is a declaration of war against darkness. Every diaper changed, every prayer whispered over your child, every sacrifice you make—it matters more than you know.

Why Some Women Are Suffering More

You're not the only one feeling this weight. Around the world, women are being pressured in different ways:

- In countries like China, women were forced to abort second children under the infamous One-Child Policy.
- In parts of Africa and Latin America, women are sterilized or coerced into family planning programs they don't fully understand.
- And here in the U.S., women are made to feel that choosing children over career is failure.

Meanwhile, in cultures where motherhood is celebrated and supported, postpartum depression is almost nonexistent. What's the difference? Support. Honor. Community. In places like India, Malaysia, and even among religious groups like the Amish or Orthodox Jews, mothers are nurtured, not judged. They are protected, not pressured. They are seen, not sidelined.

What This Means for You

If you've ever felt unseen in your motherhood… if you've felt like your dreams must shrink to fit inside your diaper bag… if you've questioned whether you're doing something wrong by having children instead of "living your life"—you are not crazy. You are living in a world that is spiritually and politically set against you.

But you are not powerless.

You are raising warriors. You are birthing legacy. You are doing holy work.

And while nations crumble under the weight of declining birth rates and broken families, you are building something eternal—one child, one prayer, one hug at a time.

God's Promise Still Stands

Don't let the world's fear replace your faith. The same God who fed manna to His people in the wilderness will provide for you and your children. You are not raising your family alone. Heaven backs you.

- "Children are a heritage from the Lord…" (Psalm 127:3)
- "Do not conform to the pattern of this world…" (Romans 12:2)

- "Are you not much more valuable than they?" (Matthew 6:26)

When the world says "enough," God says "abundance." When the world says "burden," God says "blessing."

Let's Reclaim What Was Ours All Along

It's time to take back the narrative.

- Let's stop apologizing for having children.
- Let's refuse to see motherhood as second-class.
- Let's raise our children with boldness, faith, and purpose.

Motherhood is not a crisis. It is a calling. And you, dear mother, are not just a participant in this spiritual war—you are on the front lines.

Let the world keep chasing control. You, instead, chase Christ. And in doing so, you'll raise up a generation who knows the truth, walks in faith, and defies the lies of fear-based agendas.

When you embrace motherhood, you're not just nurturing life—you're preserving legacy, planting kingdom seeds, and pushing back the darkness with every lullaby, every meal, every prayer.

Stay strong. You're not just raising children. You're raising nations.

Chapter 4:

The Genocide of Children in the Name of Progress Speaking Truth to a Mother's Heart

You carry life. You nurture it. You hold in your arms and in your womb the hope of generations. And yet, the world around you often whispers lies—about children, about your body, and about your divine purpose. It tells you that motherhood is a burden, that children are optional or expendable, that your fertility is a problem to be managed instead of a gift to be honored. This chapter is written for you. Not to shame, but to awaken; not to accuse, but to empower. Because you deserve to know what you're up against—and more importantly, what God has placed within you.

When Progress Comes at the Cost of Life

In every corner of the world, policies and ideologies have been carefully crafted to discourage motherhood and dismantle families. The destruction of children has been cloaked in terms like "choice," "liberation," and "development." But beneath those words lies a coordinated effort to stop life before it begins or to prevent it from flourishing once it has.

In China, for years, mothers were forced to choose between their children and their freedom. Millions of women endured abortions and sterilizations under the one-child policy. In India, women—many of them poor, voiceless, and vulnerable—were herded into sterilization camps, sold on the idea that fewer children meant a better life. These weren't isolated events. These were government-driven campaigns, built on fear and aimed at controlling something sacred: the womb.

Even here in our own communities, abortion is not just available—it's encouraged, subsidized, even celebrated. Organizations receive billions to promote it, especially in low-income and minority neighborhoods. This isn't progress. This is genocide disguised as empowerment. And too often, the ones most affected are women like you.

A Spiritual War on Your Seed

Mama, what you carry inside of you—the ability to create, nurture, and raise a child of God—is dangerous to the enemy. From the beginning, Satan has sought to destroy the seed of the woman. It's no coincidence that every generation has faced attacks against children. The enemy knows that every baby born could be a prophet, a preacher, a peacemaker, a world-changer.

He uses fear to make motherhood look risky. He plants doubts that sound like this:

- "What if I can't afford another child?"
- "The world is too dangerous for kids."
- "My body isn't ready for this."

But those fears are not from God. God has never asked you to provide everything—only to trust Him to provide. Philippians 4:19 promises that He will supply all your needs according to His riches. That includes your children's needs too.

Children Are Not a Problem—They Are a Promise

You may have heard people say that the world is too full. That the earth can't handle more mouths to feed. But here's the truth: scarcity is not a population issue. It's a distribution issue. God did not create a world without enough. He created a world of abundance, and then called you to multiply, not minimize.

The attack on children is not logical—it's spiritual. The more families are discouraged from growing, the more society suffers. Countries with low birth rates are now facing aging populations, worker shortages, and collapsing economies. This is what happens when the blessing of children is rejected: the future becomes uncertain.

But more than economic consequences, there are spiritual consequences. When nations permit the shedding of innocent blood, they invite judgment. Proverbs 6:16-17 says God hates hands that shed innocent blood. And there is no blood more innocent than that of a child—born or unborn.

You Are a Gatekeeper of Generations

You are not just a mother to your own children—you are a vessel for legacy. When you say yes to motherhood, you say yes to shaping the future. Every diaper changed, every tear wiped, every prayer whispered over your child is spiritual warfare. You are building a wall of faith that your children will stand on long after you are gone.

God chose you to be a mother on purpose. Not just biologically, but spiritually. In Deuteronomy 6:6-7, He calls you to teach your children diligently. That means your voice, your presence, your example—it all matters. You are not just raising babies; you are raising arrows that will fly farther than you ever could.

What Can You Do, Mama?

The enemy wants you silent. He wants you overwhelmed, worn out, and disillusioned. But you are not powerless. Here's how you can fight back:

1. Pray Like a Warrior

Intercede for the unborn. Pray for mothers who are scared and unsure. Stand in the gap for the next generation. Your prayers shift atmospheres and break chains.

2. Speak Life

Don't stay quiet. Share your story. Celebrate your children. Be the voice that counters the culture of death with declarations of life.

3. Support Other Mothers

You are not alone. And neither is she. Whether it's a meal, a ride to the doctor, or just a listening ear—your support could save a life.

4. Live Boldly and Without Fear

Trust that if God gave you a child, He has already made provision. Walk in faith, not fear. God did not make a mistake when He made you a mother.

A Final Word for Your Heart

This is not a chapter about guilt. It's a chapter about redemption and power. If you've believed the lies or walked through the pain of loss—know that God's grace is sufficient. He restores. He renews. And He can use your story to bring healing to someone else.

Mama, the seed inside you is sacred. Your children are not accidents; they are assignments. The world may call them burdens, but Heaven calls them blessings. Stand firm. Speak truth. And remember: when you protect life, you partner with God Himself.

You were made to multiply.

Chapter 5:

You Are Not Broken—Rethinking Postpartum Depression Beyond the West

You are not broken. If you've been feeling heavy, numb, or unseen since giving birth, I want you to know something: you are not crazy, and you are not alone. You may have been told that what you're feeling is postpartum depression. But what if there's more to the story? What if what you're really feeling is the weight of unmet needs, spiritual exhaustion, and the pressure to do it all alone?

In Western culture, we often rush to medicalize every emotion a mother feels after childbirth. Hormones. Imbalances. Diagnoses. Pills. But in many non-Western cultures, mothers experience the postpartum season very differently—not because their bodies are different, but because their support systems are.

Let's talk honestly about what's really going on.

You Were Never Meant to Mother Alone

In many parts of the world—Africa, Asia, the Middle East—mothers are surrounded after birth. Aunties, grandmothers, sisters, neighbors—they show up, cook, clean, carry the baby, and care for the mother. There's a rhythm of rest, ritual, and respect that allows her to heal and be seen.

Imagine what your life would feel like if you had that kind of support.

You were never meant to give everything and receive nothing. You were not created to survive this sacred journey in isolation. That's not weakness—it's design. God created community for a reason. In non-Western cultures, community is the treatment. Love and presence are the healing.

Your Emotions Are Valid—But They're Not Always Depression

Let's clear something up: feeling sad, tired, frustrated, or overwhelmed after having a baby doesn't always mean you're depressed. Sometimes it means you're sleep-deprived. Sometimes it means you need help and no one's showing up. Sometimes it means you're pouring from a cup that's been empty for months.

And sometimes, it means your soul is crying out for more— more connection, more purpose, more of God.

In the West, we've been taught to suppress that cry with medication and diagnoses. But what if those tears are a holy signal, not a symptom? What if they're calling you back to God's design—a life where you're supported, loved, and deeply anchored in Him?

Motherhood Is Not a Burden—It's a Calling

You may have been told that your value lies in your productivity—your job, your appearance, your achievements. And maybe now, in this season of diapers and dishes, you feel invisible. But hear this: God sees you. And He calls you blessed.

In many non-Western cultures, motherhood is revered, not reduced. It's seen as a spiritual honor, not a pause on life. You are raising eternity in your arms. This is not a detour. It is divine.

So no, you are not just "a mom." You are a kingdom builder. You are a nurturer of life. You are chosen for this.

When Your Soul Feels Tired

If you've lost your joy, your peace, or your sense of identity, you may be fighting a spiritual battle, not just an emotional one. The enemy loves to target mothers. He whispers that you're failing, that you're alone, that you're not enough.

But he's a liar!

You are strong.

You are equipped.

You are not forgotten.

Your healing begins by reclaiming your truth. You are a daughter of the Most High God, not defined by your struggles but by your Savior.

When your soul feels weary, come back to the Source. God is not far. He is near to the brokenhearted and binds up their wounds (Psalm 147:3).

You Deserve Help—and It's Okay to Ask

Somewhere along the line, you may have been taught that asking for help makes you weak. It doesn't. It makes you wise.

In cultures that understand this, new mothers are cared for like queens. And guess what? Those mothers experience less emotional distress—not because they're stronger, but because they're supported.

You deserve the same.

Don't wait for permission to prioritize your healing. Ask a friend to hold the baby. Let someone cook for you. Say no to things that drain you. Say yes to rest, prayer, and people who speak life over you.

You Don't Need to Be Perfect—You Need to Be Present

The world will tell you to "bounce back." But you don't need to bounce back. You need to be held.

You don't need to be a perfect mom. You need to be a present mom—a woman who is healing, growing, learning, and loving in real time.

Perfection is a myth. God is not asking for your performance— He's asking for your heart.

How to Start Healing Today

Here's what you can begin doing right now:

1. Reach out – Call a sister, a mentor, or your church family. Let someone know how you're really doing.

2. Re-center your heart – Spend time in the Word. Ask God to renew your mind. Remind yourself who you are in Him.

3. Release the guilt – It's okay to rest. It's okay to need help. It's okay to feel what you feel.

4. Receive love – From your community, from your children, from God. Let love in.

You Are Not Failing—You Are Becoming

This season is not your ending. It's part of your becoming.

Depression does not have the final word. Fear does not get to define you. Isolation is not your portion. Your story isn't over—it's being rewritten with grace, purpose, and power.

So breathe, mama. You're not broken. You're birthing something holy—not just in your child, but in yourself.

Lean into the truth. Lean into God. And let Him restore the parts of you that the world has overlooked.

You are seen.

You are called.

You are enough.

Chapter 6:

Reclaiming the Biblical Role of Motherhood – Embrace God's Design

In a world that often downplays the importance of motherhood, it's time to reclaim the truth: God designed motherhood as a sacred calling. Your role isn't just meaningful—it's powerful. You are more than a caretaker; you are a nurturer, a teacher, and a spiritual guide entrusted with shaping the next generation for God's kingdom.

This chapter will encourage mothers to see their role through God's eyes, recognizing that every diaper change, sleepless night, and teachable moment is part of a greater purpose. You are not just raising children; you are raising kingdom builders, future leaders, and warriors for Christ.

Motherhood: A Holy Assignment

God views motherhood as ministry. Every late-night feeding, every prayer whispered over your child, every act of patience is part of a divine mission. You aren't just raising children—you're raising kingdom builders, future leaders, and Christ-followers.

The Strength of a Praying Mother

There will be days when you're exhausted, afraid, or uncertain. But you're not expected to walk this journey alone. Prayer is your lifeline—your anchor in the chaos.

- When anxiety rises, Philippians 4:6 reminds you to bring everything to God in prayer.
- When wisdom is needed, James 1:5 promises God will generously provide it.
- When you feel weak, Psalm 28:7 declares that God is your strength and shield.

You don't have to have it all together. You just need to stay connected to the One who does.

Motherhood with Purpose

God entrusted you with the influence to shape hearts, minds, and destinies. Here's what that looks like:

1. Lead Spiritually

Teach your children about God not just through words, but by how you live (Deuteronomy 6:6–7). Your faith becomes their foundation.

2. Build Godly Character

Your guidance molds their values and choices. Proverbs 22:6 encourages you to train them in the right way—God's way.

3. Reflect Christ's Love

Every act of selfless care echoes Christ's love for His people. You're living out a divine example.

How to Walk Boldly in Your Calling

1. Stay Close to God

Daily time with Him fills you with strength, patience, and clarity.

2. Protect Your Marriage

A unified home creates a strong foundation for parenting. Pray and grow together as partners.

3. Live What You Teach

Let your actions show your children what it means to live for God.

4. Treasure the Moments

Don't overlook the small joys—these moments are where legacy is built.

"Her children rise up and call her blessed…" (Proverbs 31:28)

You Were Chosen for This

Motherhood is not a mistake or a setback—it's a divine assignment. Psalm 127:3 says children are a reward from the Lord. And if He gave you this role, He's also given you the grace to walk it out.

Don't believe the lie that motherhood will hold you back. In God's eyes, it propels you forward—building character, compassion, and eternal impact.

Your Influence is Generational

The seeds you plant today will bear fruit for years to come.

- Timothy's faith was nurtured by his mother and grandmother (2 Timothy 1:5).
- King Solomon's wisdom was influenced by his mother's counsel (Proverbs 31:1).

When you raise your children in faith, you're establishing a legacy the enemy can't destroy.

Simple, Powerful Ways to Raise Godly Children

- *Model faith daily* – Let them see you trust God in real life.
- *Speak life over them* – Your words shape their self-worth (Proverbs 18:21).
- *Teach God's Word* – Make Scripture part of everyday life.
- *Pray for them constantly* – Cover their journey in prayer.
- *Celebrate their purpose* – Call out their gifts and affirm their identity in Christ.

This is more than parenting—it's discipleship.

Seasons of Motherhood: God is in Each One

Whether you're cradling a newborn or guiding an adult child, your role may change, but your influence remains.

- Infancy & Early Childhood: Build a foundation of faith and love.
- Childhood & Adolescence: Teach, train, and lead by example.
- Young Adulthood: Trust God with their independence and continue to pray with confidence.

Even when they grow, your prayers still protect, your wisdom still guides, and your love still covers.

When You Feel Tired, Remember This:

- God chose you for this child.
- He equips those He calls.
- You are not just "enough"—you are chosen, anointed, and appointed.

"And let us not grow weary of doing good, for in due season we will reap, if we do not give up." (Galatians 6:9)

Motherhood is a battle worth fighting. And with God as your strength, victory is already yours.

Conclusion:

A Call to Faith, Strength, and Purpose in Motherhood

As we close this journey through the truths, trials, and triumphs of motherhood, one truth remains clear: the role of a mother is sacred, powerful, and divinely appointed. The challenges mothers face—whether emotional, spiritual, or circumstantial—do not define their worth, nor do they diminish the calling on their lives. These struggles are not permanent, and they are not your identity. Through Christ, every mother has the authority to rise above them, reclaim her purpose, and walk confidently in her God-given role.

The Reality of Struggles and the Power of Overcoming

Motherhood is both one of the greatest honors and one of the greatest challenges a woman can face. From sleepless nights and financial strain to emotional battles and societal pressures, the journey is rarely easy. But these obstacles are not proof of failure—they are proof of your strength.

What many call postpartum depression may often be the result of spiritual warfare, isolation, or unhealed trauma—real battles that require more than a diagnosis. They require discernment, faith, support, and divine intervention. You are not broken. You are not alone. And you are not powerless. With Christ, you have everything you need to rise, heal, and lead your family with grace and wisdom.

Isaiah 41:10 reminds us, "Fear not, for I am with you; be not dismayed, for I am your God. I will strengthen you, I will help you, I will uphold you with my righteous right hand."

The Power of Community

One of the greatest lies the enemy tells mothers is that they have to do it all alone. But God never intended for motherhood to be walked in isolation. Ecclesiastes 4:9-10 teaches us the value of community—where one falls, another can lift her up.

Whether through church, trusted friends, or other mothers, building a supportive village is essential. Community brings strength, encouragement, and perspective. It reminds you that you are seen, heard, and supported. In community, motherhood becomes lighter, joy is multiplied, and burdens are shared.

Reclaiming Biblical Motherhood

Throughout this book, we've shattered cultural myths and replaced them with biblical truth. From the examples of Hannah, Mary, Lois, and others, we've seen that motherhood is not just about birthing children—it's about raising kingdom leaders, building legacy, and partnering with God in one of the most important assignments on Earth.

You are not just a caretaker. You are a warrior. A teacher. A disciple-maker. Your work is holy. Your influence is eternal. As Titus 2:3-5 shows us, this is a generational calling. When mothers pour into each other, they raise up strong, godly homes that echo into the future.

Living Out Your God-Given Purpose

Motherhood is not a mistake or a secondary calling—it is divine purpose. Whether you're raising children full-time, balancing work and home, or nurturing children through a different season of life, God has positioned you to influence lives for His glory.

Ground yourself in Christ. Let your identity flow from Him—not your past, not your pain, not the world's opinion. You are victorious. You are chosen. You are more than a conqueror (Romans 8:37).

You are:

- A warrior in God's army, shaping the future.
- A teacher, pouring wisdom into young hearts.
- A disciple-maker, fulfilling the Great Commission within your home.

Whatever your journey has looked like—whether marked by joy, loss, confusion, or breakthrough—know this: God chose you for this moment. Walk boldly. You are fully equipped. Your labor is not in vain.

"She is clothed with strength and dignity; she can laugh at the days to come." – Proverbs 31:25

Hope for the Future: A Legacy of Faith and Love

As this book comes to an end, may a new beginning take place in your heart. May you walk forward with fresh strength, clear purpose, and unwavering hope. What you do as a mother matters deeply. The prayers you pray, the love you give, the truth you teach—it's all building something greater than you can imagine.

You are planting seeds of faith that will blossom for generations. You are shaping legacy. You are changing eternity, one day, one child, one prayer at a time.

Final Words of Encouragement

Motherhood is a journey of trust, surrender, and relentless love. There will be hard days, but there will also be days filled with joy, laughter, peace, and purpose. Don't let discouragement have the final word—let faith rise.

God sees you.

God is with you.

And God is using you.

Stand tall, mama. You are part of something divine.

"May you be strengthened with all power, according to His glorious might, for all endurance and patience with joy." – Colossians 1:11

This is your story. A story of faith. A story of strength. A story of motherhood redeemed and empowered—for the glory of God.

Closing Prayer: A Mother's Prayer of Strength and Surrender

Heavenly Father,

Thank You for the sacred calling of motherhood. Thank You for entrusting me with the lives of these precious children and for walking beside me through every high and every low. Lord, I surrender every fear, every failure, every tear, and every unanswered question at Your feet. Strengthen me for the journey ahead.

Remind me daily that I am not alone. That even when I feel unseen, You see me. Even when I feel unheard, You hear every cry of my heart. And even when I feel weak, You are my strength.

Help me to walk boldly in my identity as Your daughter and as the mother You've called me to be. Silence the lies of the enemy that try to tell me I'm not enough. Uproot every seed of doubt, fear, or shame. Fill me instead with peace, wisdom, and unshakable faith.

God, create in me a clean heart, renew my mind, and restore the joy of motherhood. Help me to love well, lead with grace, and model faith that my children will carry into future generations.

Lord, I ask for divine protection over my family, supernatural provision in times of lack, and Holy Spirit guidance in every decision. Surround me with a godly community. Let my life and my motherhood bring You glory.

I trust You with this calling. I trust You with my children. And I trust You with my story.

In Yeshua's name,

Amen.

Appendix:
Practical Tools and Resources for Embracing Motherhood with Faith, Strength, and Purpose

As a mother, embracing the full scope of your God-given role is not only about understanding the spiritual truths we've discussed, but also about equipping yourself with practical tools and resources. In this appendix, we aim to provide practical, actionable steps and resources to help you thrive in your journey of motherhood, whether you're facing challenges, seeking growth, or striving to nurture your family with purpose and faith. Below, you will find strategies for managing the demands of motherhood, connecting with your faith, and supporting your well-being.

1. Practical Tools for Managing Mental and Emotional Well-Being

a. Daily Devotions and Prayer

Spending time with God is essential for nurturing both your spiritual and emotional health. Establishing a daily routine of prayer and Bible reading can provide the strength you need to overcome the challenges of motherhood and connect deeply with your calling.

Actionable Tips:

- **Set a consistent time for daily devotionals**: Whether it's early in the morning before your children wake up or during their nap time, carve out time for personal Bible study and prayer.
- **Devotional book:** Set time to write in 30-day devotional book in following section each day.
- **Prayer journal**: Writing out your prayers can be an excellent way to process emotions, track spiritual growth, and see God's faithfulness in your life.
- **Prayer cards**: Read the 30-day prayer cards supplied for you in following section each day.

b. Practice Gratitude

Gratitude can be a powerful tool in combating feelings of depression and overwhelm. By focusing on what you're thankful for, you shift your mindset from a place of scarcity to one of abundance, helping to transform your emotional state.

Actionable Tips:

- **Start a gratitude journal**: Every evening, write down at least three things you're grateful for that day, whether it's something small or significant. Over time, this helps train your mind to focus on the positive.
- **Encourage family gratitude**: At dinner or bedtime, ask your children to share something they are thankful for. This creates a culture of gratitude in the home and strengthens family bonds.

c. Build Emotional Resilience

Motherhood often brings emotional ups and downs. Learning how to build emotional resilience will help you better navigate the hard days and stay grounded in your faith.

Actionable Tips:

- **Recognize your emotional triggers**: Understanding what causes stress or frustration in your life (e.g., lack of sleep, overwhelming tasks, or lack of support) can help you proactively address these stressors.
- **Develop coping strategies**: Whether it's taking deep breaths, going for a walk, or listening to worship music, find methods

that help you calm your mind and recenter yourself when emotions feel overwhelming.

- **Seek professional support if necessary**: If you're struggling with emotional health and feel unable to manage on your own, consider seeking support from a counselor or therapist who shares your faith values.

2. Building a Supportive Community and Networking

No mother should walk this journey alone. A strong community provides encouragement, practical help, and accountability. It also creates a space for mothers to share their struggles and joys, learning from one another.

a. Finding or Starting a Moms Group

A mom's group can be an invaluable support system. It provides the opportunity to share experiences, receive advice, and offer encouragement in a safe and welcoming environment.

Actionable Tips:

- **Join or start a Bible study for mothers**: Look for a group in your church or community that focuses on biblical teachings about motherhood. If one doesn't exist, consider starting one with a few like-minded mothers. If you are in the Hampton

Roads Area of Virginia, "*A Breath of Life Women's Ministry*" host multiple events each year for mothers. Look us up on social media (Facebook & Instagram) or email us at: ABreathofLifeWomensMinisty@yahoo.com for upcoming events.

- **Engage in online communities**: There are numerous faith-based groups online where mothers can connect, share resources, and pray for one another, such as *A Breath of Life Women's Ministry, Moms in Prayer, Mama Get Up!,* or *The Mom Life* Facebook groups.

- **Attend a mothering conference or retreat**: These events can offer refreshment, fellowship, and teaching that will equip you to better navigate your role as a mother.

b. Building a Supportive Spouse Relationship

Your relationship with your spouse is foundational to your emotional health and the well-being of your family. Strong marriages are built on communication, trust, and shared values.

Actionable Tips:

- **Date nights and intentional time together**: Even amidst the busyness of raising children, it's vital to prioritize your marriage. Plan regular date nights or create small, meaningful moments of connection.

- **Communication and emotional support**: Be open with your spouse about your struggles and needs. This helps avoid misunderstandings and builds mutual respect and support.

3. Developing Healthy Routines for Physical and Mental Health

Physical health plays a crucial role in mental and emotional well-being. Developing routines that prioritize both your physical and mental health will equip you to thrive as a mother.

a. Sleep and Rest

One of the most significant challenges mothers face, particularly with infants and young children, is getting enough rest. Lack of sleep can contribute to feelings of overwhelm, irritability, and even depression.

Actionable Tips:

- **Prioritize sleep**: Create a routine where you go to bed at the same time every night. Sleep is essential to your well-being and your ability to care for your family.
- **Nap when possible**: If your child naps, take that time to rest as well. Even a 15-30 minute power nap can help replenish your energy.

- **Use rest as an act of worship**: Understand that God commands rest and use your moments of respite to thank Him for your ability to rest and recharge (Exodus 34:21).

b. Exercise and Movement

Regular physical activity not only benefits your body but also improves your mood by releasing endorphins, which help reduce stress and anxiety.

Actionable Tips:

- **Daily movement**: Incorporate movement into your daily routine, whether it's a walk, stretching, yoga, or a fitness class. Exercise can be a great way to clear your mind and relieve stress.
- **Include your children in activities**: If you have young children, consider family-friendly activities like walks, bike rides, or playing in the park that can get you moving while spending quality time together.

c. Nutrition

Eating a balanced diet can impact how you feel mentally and emotionally. Proper nutrition supports your brain function, energy levels, and overall mood.

Actionable Tips:

- **Plan meals ahead**: When possible, plan and prepare meals in advance to reduce the mental load during the week. Healthy meals fuel your body, and a well-balanced diet can improve your mood and energy.
- **Snack wisely**: Choose snacks that boost your energy and improve mental clarity, such as fruits, nuts, and protein-rich snacks.
- **Hydrate**: Drinking enough water throughout the day helps maintain your physical health and mental sharpness.

4. Spiritual Practices for Strengthening Faith

A strong relationship with God is the bedrock of overcoming the challenges of motherhood. The following spiritual practices can help you stay grounded in God's Word and His promises.

a. Meditation on Scripture

Taking time each day to meditate on Scripture will nourish your spirit and keep you aligned with God's purpose for your life.

Actionable Tips:

- **Scripture memory**: Memorize key verses that speak to your identity in Christ, your role as a mother, and your calling as a woman of faith. Verses like Proverbs 31:25-28, Isaiah 40:29-31, and Philippians 4:6-7 can provide strength during difficult times.

- **Read the Bible aloud**: Whether alone or with your children, reading Scripture aloud can help both you and your family feel connected to God's Word.

b. Worship and Praise

Incorporating worship into your daily routine can shift your perspective, helping you to find joy and strength even in the midst of challenges.

Actionable Tips:

- **Worship through music**: Create a playlist of worship songs that uplift your spirit. Sing along while doing chores, driving, or during quiet moments.
- **Praise God for the little victories**: Celebrate each day as a gift from God. Even on the tough days, finding moments to praise Him will help you remember His goodness.

c. Acts of Service

Motherhood itself is an act of service. Serving others, whether through volunteer work, helping a neighbor, or supporting fellow mothers, can bring joy and a sense of purpose.

Actionable Tips:

- **Serve in your church**: Whether you can serve in a nursery, organize a women's event, or join a ministry team, find ways to contribute to your church community.
- **Serve others with your children**: Teach your children the importance of serving others by involving them in charitable acts, whether it's helping a neighbor or giving to a cause you care about.

grace in the CHAOS

Daily Devotions
r the Busy Mom

Apostle Latina Campbell

Welcome to Grace in the Chaos: Daily Refreshment for Mothers, a 30-day devotional designed specifically for busy moms who are seeking moments of spiritual renewal amidst their hectic days. Each day, we'll explore scriptures that speak directly to the heart of motherhood, offering insights and encouragement to help you navigate the challenges and joys of raising children while deepening your relationship with God.

As you journey through this devotional, you'll find daily Bible verses, reflective passages, prayers, and simple actions designed to fit into your busy schedule, yet powerful enough to bring significant changes to your daily life. Whether you're dealing with toddler tantrums, teenage angst, or the balancing act of work and family life, these pages aim to provide you with a dose of grace and peace that will uplift and strengthen you.

This guide is more than just a reading plan; it's a companion for your spiritual journey as a mother. It's here to remind you that in the midst of chaos, there is grace—abundant, life-giving grace that God freely offers to help you manage every day with faith and love. Let's embrace this journey together, finding joy and peace in the promises of God, and refreshing our spirits in His presence.

Embracing Peace in the Midst of Chaos

John 16:33 - I have told you these things, so that in me you may have peace. In this world you will have trouble. But take heart! I have overcome the world.

———————

In the whirlwind of daily responsibilities, finding peace might seem elusive. Jesus assures us that despite the inevitable challenges we face, His presence brings peace that transcends understanding. As you navigate the chaos of motherhood, remember that His strength is perfect when our strength is insufficient.

How can you cultivate a habit of seeking Christ's peace daily?

_____

_____

_____

_____

_____

_____

_____

Gods Strength in Your Weakness

2 Corinthians 12:9 - But he said to me, 'My grace is sufficien
for you, for my power is made perfect in weakness.'
Therefore I will boast all the more gladly about my
weaknesses, so that Christ's power may rest on me.

It's easy to feel inadequate in our roles as mothers, but God's power is most evident when we feel most incapable. His grace not only covers our shortcomings but empowers us to handle what we could not on our own. Today, embrace your weaknesses as opportunities for God to display His strength.

How does acknowledging your weaknesses change your reliance on God's strength?

_____

_____

_____

_____

_____

_____

_____

_____

Finding Joy in Motherhood

Psalm 113:9 - He settles the childless woman in her home as a happy mother of children. Praise the Lord.

Motherhood is a mix of joy and challenges. The Scripture reminds us that children are a blessing from the Lord. Today, focus on the joy that comes from God through your role as a mother, seeing your children as blessings that bring happiness and fulfillment.

What aspects of motherhood bring you the most joy, and how can you celebrate these more often?

_____

_____

_____

_____

_____

_____

_____

_____

Wisdom in Parenting

James 1:5 - If any of you lacks wisdom, you should ask God, who gives generously to all without finding fault, and it will be given to you.

Parenting requires wisdom beyond our own understanding. God promises to provide that wisdom liberally when we ask. As you face decisions big and small in raising your children, turn to God first, trusting that He will guide you in every step.

How has seeking God's wisdom in parenting made a difference in your family?

_____

_____

_____

_____

_____

_____

_____

Prayer in Chaos

Philippians 4:6-7 - Do not be anxious about anything, but in every situation, by prayer and petition, with thanksgiving, present your requests to God. And the peace of God, which transcends all understanding, will guard your hearts and your minds in Christ Jesus

———————

In the hectic pace of motherhood, it's vital to anchor your day in prayer. Communicating with God brings peace that can calm any chaos. Today, let every worry be a prompt to pray, turning your anxieties into conversations with God.

What changes when you replace worry with prayer?

_____

_____

_____

_____

_____

_____

_____

Resting in God's Promises

Matthew 11:28 - Come to me, all you who are weary and burdened, and I will give you rest.

Motherhood can be exhausting, but Jesus offers us a rest that rejuvenates our souls. Trust in His promises to provide rest when you feel burdened by the demands of life. Let His strength and peace be your refuge.

How can you more regularly incorporate physical and spiritual rest into your routine?

_____

_____

_____

_____

_____

_____

_____

Cultivating a Spirit of Patience

Colossians 3:12 – Therefore, as God's chosen people, holy and dearly loved, clothe yourselves with compassion, kindness, humility, gentleness and patience.

Patience is a virtue often stretched thin in parenting, yet it is crucial for fostering a loving environment. God calls us to model patience, reflecting His character to our children. Seek to cultivate this fruit of the Spirit in your interactions today.

What triggers impatience in you, and how can you more effectively manage these triggers?

_____

_____

_____

_____

_____

_____

_____

Strength to Persevere

Isaiah 40:29 - He gives strength to the weary and increases the power of the weak.

As a mom, there are days when you feel completely drained, both physically and emotionally. It's in these moments of exhaustion that God's promise to give strength to the weary shines as a beacon of hope. He understands your tiredness and stands ready to supply the energy you cannot muster on your own. Turn to Him when the coffee isn't enough, and the sleep is too little. Let His endless energy fill you and transform your fatigue into fortitude. God's strength is perfect and precisely portioned for the days when your strength falls short.

How can recognizing God's provision of strength change your approach to challenging days?

_____

_____

_____

_____

_____

_____

_____

_____

Loving Through Conflict

Ephesians 4:2-3 - Be completely humble and gentle; be patient, bearing with one another in love. Make every effort to keep the unity of the Spirit through the bond of peace.

Conflict is inevitable in any family, especially as children grow and develop their own opinions and personalities. Navigating these conflicts with grace can be challenging but is essential for maintaining a loving home environment. God calls us to respond with humility, gentleness, and patience, tools that are more effective than anger and sharp words. By embodying these virtues, you reflect Christ's love and teach your children how to handle disagreements in a godly manner. This approach not only resolves conflicts more peacefully but also strengthens the bonds of love and respect within the family.

What difference does it make when you handle conflicts with gentleness and patience?

_____

_____

_____

_____

_____

_____

_____

Embracing the Role of a Teacher

Proverbs 22:6 - Start children off on the way they should go, and even when they are old they will not turn from it.

Every day, you are teaching your children, whether it's academically, spiritually, or socially. Your role as their first and most influential teacher is a profound responsibility bestowed by God. Embrace this role with intentionality, understanding that the lessons you impart will help shape their futures. Teach them about kindness, honesty, and the love of Christ. Remember, the most impactful lessons are often caught rather than taught; how you live and react daily is as powerful as the words you speak.

What are the most important values or lessons you want to teach your children, and how are you modeling these?

_____

_____

_____

_____

_____

_____

_____

_____

Finding Fulfillment in Motherhood

Psalm 127:3 - Children are a heritage from the Lord, offspring a reward from him.

It's easy to get caught up in the daily grind of parenting and miss the profound joy and fulfillment that comes with being a mom. Recognize that your children are gifts from God, entrusted to you to love, nurture, and raise. Cherish the small moments just as much as the significant milestones. Seek joy in the mundane parts of motherhood by viewing them through the lens of eternal impact. Cultivating a heart of gratitude for the opportunity to mother these souls can transform your perspective and infuse your daily routine with divine purpose.

How does viewing your children as gifts from God change your daily perspective?

_____

_____

_____

_____

_____

_____

_____

_____

the Importance of Self-Care

Mark 6:31 - Then, because so many people were coming and going that they did not even have a chance to eat, he said to them, 'Come with me by yourselves to a quiet place and get some rest.'

In the busyness of mothering, taking time for yourself can seem impossible or even selfish. However, Jesus Himself emphasized the importance of rest and retreat for renewal. Taking time to care for yourself isn't just necessary; it's a biblical principle that allows you to recharge and continue serving your family with energy and love. Whether it's a few moments alone with a book, a quiet morning walk, or a night out with friends, prioritizing self-care is crucial for maintaining your physical, emotional, and spiritual health.

What changes do you notice in your ability to parent effectively when you prioritize self-care?

_____

_____

_____

_____

_____

_____

_____

_____

Sustaining a Marriage in Parenthood

Ecclesiastes 4:12 - Though one may be overpowered, two can defend themselves. A cord of three strands is not quickly broken

---

While parenting can sometimes consume all your energy and focus, sustaining your marriage is crucial. A healthy partnership provides stability and a loving environment for your children. It's important to nurture your relationship with your spouse, making time for each other amidst the demands of parenting. Pray together, go on dates, and keep communication open. Remember, a strong marriage not only benefits you and your spouse but also provides a secure foundation for your children.

How can you better balance the roles of being both a spouse and a parent?

_____

_____

_____

_____

_____

_____

_____

_____

Weekly Reflection and Prayer

Lamentations 3:22-23 - Because of the Lord's great lov
we are not consumed, for his compassions never fail.
They are new every morning; great is your faithfulness

As this week comes to a close, take some time to reflect on the lessons learned and the moments you've experienced God's grace. Acknowledge the challenges but also celebrate the victories, no matter how small. Use this day to recharge spiritually, setting goals for the coming week and committing them to the Lord in prayer. Reflect on the growth in your faith, the strength in your relationships, and the joy in motherhood.

What are the most significant ways you've seen God move in your life this week?

_____

_____

_____

_____

_____

_____

_____

_____

Patience in Parenting

James 1:19 - Everyone should be quick to listen, slow to speak and slow to become angry.

Patience is a virtue that is often tested in the whirlwind of motherhood. It requires us to take a deep breath and choose a measured response over a reactive one. Remember, your children are not just tasks to manage but little people to nurture and guide. Emulating patience teaches them how to handle their own frustrations and challenges gracefully. When you feel your patience waning, pause and ask God to refill you with His peace and understanding.

How does practicing patience affect the atmosphere of your home?

_____

_____

_____

_____

_____

_____

_____

_____

Grace in Discipline

Hebrews 12:11 - No discipline seems pleasant at the time, bu painful. Later on, however, it produces a harvest of righteousn and peace for those who have been trained by it.

Discipline is an essential aspect of parenting, though often misunderstood. It's not about punishment, but about guiding and teaching. Approaching discipline with grace means looking beyond the immediate behavior to the long-term growth and learning of your child. Let your discipline actions be firm but loving, always aiming to instruct rather than to retaliate.

How does disciplining with grace differ from your initial instincts when correcting your children?

_____

_____

_____

_____

_____

_____

_____

_____

Encouraging Spiritual Growth in Children

Deuteronomy 11:19 - Teach them to your children, talking about them when you sit at home and when you walk along the road, when you lie down and when you get u

---

Your role in nurturing your children's faith is pivotal. Incorporate spiritual teachings into everyday moments, not just during Sunday school or bedtime prayers. Let faith conversations be as natural as discussions about their day at school. This constant, casual inclusion of spiritual topics will help your children see faith as a vital, everyday part of life.

What practical steps can you take to make spiritual discussions a regular part of your family's routine?

_____

_____

_____

_____

_____

_____

_____

Overcoming Exhaustion

Isaiah 40:31 - But those who hope in the Lord will renew their strength. They will soar on wings like eagles; they wil run and not grow weary, they will walk and not be faint.

Exhaustion can make every small task feel insurmountable. Yet, Scripture promises that placing our hope in the Lord renews our strength. When you feel overwhelmed, lean on God's infinite energy. Visualize your spirit soaring like an eagle above the chaos, sustained by faith and not by your own limited endurance. It's easy to forget when you're in the thick of the mom life that you have a Heavenly Father there for you and with you in times of need.

How does trusting in God's strength help you manage physical tiredness?

_____

_____

_____

_____

_____

_____

_____

_____

Cultivating a Heart of Contentment

Philippians 4:11-12 - I have learned to be content whatever the circumstances. I know what it is to be in need, and I know what it is to have plenty. I have learned the secret of being content in any and every situation, whether well fed or hungry, whether living in plenty or in wan

---

Contentment in motherhood is not about perfect circumstances but maintaining a peaceful heart amidst the imperfections. It's about finding joy in the laughter of your children, peace in the midst of a messy home, and grace for yourself when things don't go as planned. Embrace each day not for its perfection but for the opportunities it presents. It's important to remember that there are seasons of life- ones where the house isn't as tidy as you'd like it to be but where children are busy leaving footprints all around.

What changes when you shift your focus from what your life lacks to the blessings you have?

_____

_____

_____

_____

_____

_____

_____

Nurturing Relationships Outside of Motherhood

Ecclesiastes 4:9-10 - Two are better than one, because they have a good return for their labor: If either of them falls down, one can help the other up. But pity anyone who falls and has no one to help them up.

While motherhood is a significant part of your identity, maintaining relationships outside of this role is crucial for your well-being. Friendships provide support, perspective, and relief from the insular world of parenting. Invest time in nurturing friendships that refresh and encourage you, remembering that you are not just a mom—you are a friend, a sister, a daughter, and so much more. For one day, those children won't be romping around the living room and you will have these relationships to lean in to.

How do your friendships enrich your life and help you be a better mom?

_____

_____

_____

_____

_____

_____

_____

_____

Weekly Reflection and Prayer

John 16:33 - I have told you these things, so that in me you may have peace. In this world you will have trouble. But take heart! I have overcome the world.

As another week concludes, take time today to reflect on the moments where you felt God's presence. Consider the challenges and how you faced them with grace. Use this day for spiritual reflection and to set intentions for the coming week, seeking God's guidance for continuous growth and peace.

What were the most significant spiritual lessons from this week, and how will they influence your upcoming week?

_____

_____

_____

_____

_____

_____

_____

Seeking Solitude for Spiritual Renewal

Mark 1:35 - Very early in the morning, while it was still dark, Jesus got up, left the house and went off to a solitary place, where he prayed.

In the busyness of motherhood, finding time for solitude can be challenging, yet it is essential for spiritual renewal. Jesus Himself sought quiet places to connect with the Father. Carve out moments in your day for stillness, whether it's early in the morning, during a child's nap, or after bedtime. These moments of solitude are vital for recharging your spiritual batteries and maintaining a close relationship with God.

How does spending time alone with God impact your day and your interactions with others?

_____

_____

_____

_____

_____

_____

_____

_____

The Importance of Patience & Perspective

Romans 12:12 – Be joyful in hope, patient in affliction, faithful in prayer.

Patience is not just a virtue to aspire to; it's a practical approach that can transform challenging moments into opportunities for growth. In the midst of tantrums or teenage rebellion, maintaining a perspective of patience allows you to respond rather than react. Remember, this season of intense mothering is just that—a season. Keeping a long-term perspective helps you to see beyond the immediate chaos. While looking into perspective, it's vital to remember that everyone has their own reality and it helps to lean into and understand others.

How does maintaining a long-term perspective change your response to daily challenges?

_____

_____

_____

_____

_____

_____

_____

_____

the Power of Encouragement

1 Thessalonians 5:11 - Therefore encourage one anothe and build each other up, just as in fact you are doing.

_____

As a mother, your words have the power to shape your children's self-esteem and worldview. Focus on using your words to encourage and affirm your children today. Celebrate their strengths and achievements, however small. Your encouragement not only boosts their confidence but also helps them to see themselves through God's eyes.

What changes do you notice in your children's behavior and in the atmosphere of your home when you focus on encouragement?

_____

_____

_____

_____

_____

_____

_____

_____

Embracing Grace in Parenting

2 Corinthians 12:9 - But he said to me, 'My grace is sufficient for you, for my power is made perfect in weakness.' Therefore I will boast all the more gladly about my weaknesses, so that Christ's power may rest on me.

———

Parenting can sometimes feel like a series of missteps and missed opportunities. It's crucial to remember that God's grace covers all our imperfections. Embrace His grace daily, allowing it to free you from guilt and empower you to parent with God's strength. When you stumble, let His grace pick you back up and guide your next steps. You are not in this alone, as God walks besides you always.

How does embracing God's grace change your approach to parenting and self-assessment?

_____

_____

_____

_____

_____

_____

_____

Modeling Faith Through Actions

James 2:18 - But someone will say, 'You have faith; I have deeds.' Show me your faith without deeds, and I will show you my faith by my deeds.

 Actions often speak louder than words, especially to children. Your daily actions are a powerful testimony of your faith to your family. By living out your beliefs, you provide a real-life example of faith in action. Let your actions today—from how you handle stress to how you treat strangers—be consistent with your Christian beliefs. Little eyes are watching- teenagers are watching. Make it a priority to understand that you are seen through a magnifying glass by your children.

How do your actions teach your children about faith?

_____

_____

_____

_____

_____

_____

_____

_____

eeking Wisdom Daily

Proverbs 2:6 - For the Lord gives wisdom; from his mouth come knowledge and understanding.

It's easy to get caught up in the responsibilities and challenges of motherhood and lose sight of the joy it can bring. Remember, the joy of the Lord is your strength. Seek to find joy not just in the milestones but in the everyday moments—the messy breakfasts, the bedtime stories, and even the laundry piles. Each of these moments is an opportunity to experience God's ongoing work in your life.

What simple changes can you make to cultivate more joy in your daily parenting tasks?

_____

_____

_____

_____

_____

_____

_____

Maintaining Joy in Motherhood

Nehemiah 8:10 - Nehemiah said, 'Go and enjoy choice food and sweet drinks, and send some to those who have nothing prepared. This day is holy to our Lord. Do not grieve, for the joy of the Lord is your strength.'

It's easy to get caught up in the responsibilities and challenges of motherhood and lose sight of the joy it can bring. Remember, the joy of the Lord is your strength. Seek to find joy not just in the milestones but in the everyday moments—the messy breakfasts, the bedtime stories, and even the laundry piles. Each of these moments is an opportunity to experience God's ongoing work in your life. Take a step back and think of all there is to be thankful for- those little feet that leave those dirty footprints and the dirty clothing that covers healthy kids.

What simple changes can you make to cultivate more joy in your daily parenting tasks?

_____

_____

_____

_____

_____

_____

_____

_____

The Value of Quiet Time

Psalm 46:10 - Be still, and know that I am God; I will be exalted among the nations, I will be exalted in the earth.

Amid the noise and busyness of family life, finding time to be still in God's presence can seem impossible. Yet, it's in these quiet moments that we often hear God's voice most clearly. Value and prioritize this time, even if it's just a few minutes each day. Let these moments of stillness refresh your soul and renew your spirit. This is a good practice to have and to exemplify to your children- that a relationship with God is priority.

How does spending quiet time with God impact your day?

_____

_____

_____

_____

_____

_____

_____

_____

Celebrating Growth and Setting New Goals

2 Peter 3:18 - "But grow in the grace and knowledge of our Lord and Savior Jesus Christ. To him be glory both now and forever! Amen.

As this devotional journey concludes, take time to celebrate the growth you've experienced over the past month. Reflect on the ways you've seen God work in your life and through your parenting. Set new spiritual goals for the coming months. Maybe it's deepening your Bible study, increasing family prayer time, or serving together as a family. Whatever it is, commit it to God and step forward with confidence and faith.

What are your spiritual goals moving forward, and how do you plan to achieve them?

_____

_____

_____

_____

_____

_____

_____

Prayer Card: Day 1

Lord Jesus, grant me peace in the midst of the daily chaos. Remind me that You are sovereign over every aspect of my life. Help me to rest in Your victorious right hand. Amen.

Grace in the CHAOS

Prayer Card: Day 2

Heavenly Father, thank You for Your power that works best in my weakness. Help me to rely on You more fully and to see my limitations as opportunities for Your strength to shine. Amen.

Grace in the CHA

Prayer Card: Day 3

Lord, thank You for the blessing of my children. Help me to find joy every day in the role You have entrusted to me as their mother. Fill our home with Your love and joy. Amen.

Grace in the CHAOS

Prayer Card: Day 4

Almighty God, I ask for Your wisdom in parenting my children. Show me how to guide them well, making decisions that reflect Your love and truth. Amen.

Grace in the CHAC

Prayer Card: Day 5

Heavenly Father, help me to bring every worry to You in prayer. Replace my anxiety with Your peace that passes all understanding. Guard my heart and mind in Christ. Amen.

Grace in the CHAOS

Prayer Card: Day 6

Lord Jesus, I come to You weary and burdened. I accept Your offer of rest. Rejuvenate my spirit and refresh my body as I trust in Your sustaining power. Amen.

Grace in the CHAO

Prayer Card: Day 7

Father, clothe me with patience as I interact with my family today. Help me to respond with gentleness and to reflect Your love in all that I do. Amen.

Grace in the CHAOS

Prayer Card: Day 8

Father, I am weary, but I look to You for strength. Infuse my days with Your power and make my weak moments strong. Help me to rely on Your energy rather than my own. Amen.

Grace in the CHAO

Prayer Card: Day 9

Lord, help me to handle conflicts within my family with humility and patience. Teach me to respond in love, preserving peace and unity at home. Amen.

Grace in the CHAOS

Prayer Card: Day 10

Heavenly Father, guide me in teaching my children. Let my words and actions consistently reflect Your truth and love. Equip me to be a godly example they can follow. Amen.

Grace in the CHA

Prayer Card: Day 11

Dear God, thank You for the gift of my children. Help me to see motherhood as a fulfilling role and to cherish each moment I have with my children. Amen.

Grace in the CHAOS

Prayer Card: Day 12

Lord, remind me of the importance of self-care and guide me to find moments for rest and rejuvenation. Help me to maintain my health so I can be the mother You've called me to be. Amen.

Grace in the CHAO

Prayer Card: Day 13

Heavenly Father, help me to nurture my marriage even as I care for my children. Strengthen our partnership and keep our bond strong and loving. Amen.

Grace in the CHAOS

Prayer Card: Day 14

Lord, as I reflect on this past week, I see Your hand in every part of my life. Help me to continue recognizing Your presence daily. Guide my intentions and actions as I move forward into another week. Amen.

Grace in the CHAO

Prayer Card: Day 15

Father, grant me patience in my interactions with my children today. Help me to listen more, speak gently, and avoid quick anger. Amen.

Grace in the CHAOS

Prayer Card: Day 16

Lord, help me to discipline with grace, keeping my child's growth and character development at the forefront of my actions. Teach me to correct with love. Amen.

Grace in the CHAC

Prayer Card: Day 17

Heavenly Father, guide me in fostering my children's spiritual growth. Help me find natural opportunities to weave Your truths into our daily conversations. Amen.

Grace in the CHAOS

Prayer Card: Day 18

Lord, I place my hope in You to renew my strength. Help me to rise above the daily exhaustion and to serve my family with renewed energy and joy. Amen.

Grace in the CHAC

Prayer Card: Day 19

Heavenly Father, teach me to find contentment in my role as a mother. Help me to appreciate the beauty of my ordinary days and find Your peace amidst the chaos. Amen.

Grace in the CHAOS

Prayer Card: Day 20

God, thank You for the gift of friendship. Help me to invest in relationships that strengthen and refresh me. Remind me of the value of maintaining connections outside of my immediate family. Amen.

Grace in the CHA

Prayer Card: Day 21

Lord, thank You for Your faithfulness this past week. As I reflect on Your love and provision, renew my spirit and prepare my heart for what lies ahead. Continue to guide me in all aspects of my life. Amen.

Grace in the CHAOS

Prayer Card: Day 22

Father, help me to find moments of solitude where I can connect with You deeply. Teach me to prioritize these precious times of prayer and reflection. Amen.

Grace in the CHAC

Prayer Card: Day 23

Lord, grant me patience in every challenging moment I face as a mom. Help me to keep a heavenly perspective, seeing beyond the temporary struggles. Amen.

Grace in the CHAOS

Prayer Card: Day 24

Heavenly Father, let my words be filled with encouragement and love today. Help me to build up my children and those around me with affirming and positive speech. Amen.

Grace in the CHAO

Prayer Card: Day 25

Lord, thank You for Your grace that covers every mistake. Help me to rely on Your strength and wisdom in every aspect of parenting. Amen.

Grace in the CHAOS

Prayer Card: Day 26

Father, help my actions to reflect my faith authentically. May my life be a testament to Your love and grace. Guide me in teaching my children by example. Amen.

Grace in the CHAO

Prayer Card: Day 27

Almighty God, I ask for Your wisdom in every decision I make as a parent. Fill me with Your knowledge and understanding. Amen.

Grace in the CHAOS

Prayer Card: Day 28

Lord, help me to find joy in the journey of motherhood. May Your joy be my strength on the hard days and my song on the good days. Amen.

Grace in the CHA

Prayer Card: Day 29

Heavenly Father, remind me of the importance of being still in Your presence. Help me to make this quiet time a priority, no matter how busy life gets. Amen.

Grace in the CHAOS

Prayer Card: Day 30

Lord, thank You for guiding me through this devotional journey. Help me to shine Your light brightly, that others may be drawn to You through my life. Empower me to disciple others as I continue to follow You. Amen.

Grace in the CHAO[...]

Grace in the Chaos Calendar

SUN	MON	TUE	WED	THU	FRI	SAT
TAKE FIVE MINUTES TO SIT IN SILENCE, FOCUSING ON THE PEACE THAT JESUS OFFERS.	PRAY FOR STRENGTH WHEN FEELING OVERWHELMED TODAY.	LIST THREE THINGS YOU'RE GRATEFUL FOR ABOUT EACH CHILD.	PAUSE AND PRAY FOR WISDOM BEFORE MAKING SIGNIFICANT DECISIONS TODAY.	STOP AND PRAY EACH TIME YOU FEEL ANXIOUS TODAY.	TAKE A NAP OR ENGAGE IN A RESTFUL ACTIVITY.	COUNT TO TEN BEFORE RESPONDING DURING MOMENTS OF FRUSTRATION.
PAUSE AND ASK GOD FOR STRENGTH WHEN FEELING TIRED TODAY.	RESPOND GENTLY IN A SITUATION WHERE YOU'D USUALLY FEEL FRUSTRATED.	DISCUSS A SPIRITUAL TRUTH OR BIBLE STORY WITH YOUR CHILDREN.	LIST THINGS YOU ARE GRATEFUL FOR AS A MOTHER.	SCHEDULE 30 MINUTES OF 'ME TIME' FOR REJUVENATION.	PLAN A DATE NIGHT OR SPECIAL TIME WITH YOUR SPOUSE.	REVIEW THE PAST WEEK AND NOTE WHERE YOU'VE SEEN GOD WORK.
COUNT TO TEN BEFORE RESPONDING TO FRUSTRATION.	REFLECT ON A DISCIPLINE SCENARIO; CONSIDER A MORE GRACEFUL APPROACH.	SHARE A BIBLE STORY OR TESTIMONY WITH YOUR CHILDREN TODAY.	PRAY FOR SPIRITUAL AND PHYSICAL REJUVENATION WHEN FEELING TIRED.	FIND GRATITUDE IN A FRUSTRATING PART OF YOUR DAY.	REACH OUT TO A FRIEND AND RECONNECT.	SPEND QUIET TIME REFLECTING ON THE PAST WEEK AND PLANNING AHEAD.
SCHEDULE TIME TODAY FOR SOLITUDE WITH PRAYER OR SCRIPTURE READING.	REMIND YOURSELF THAT THIS DIFFICULT SEASON IS TEMPORARY.	GIVE EACH CHILD A HEARTFELT COMPLIMENT TODAY.	FORGIVE YOURSELF FOR A PARENTING MISTAKE, AND PRAY FOR GUIDANCE.	SHOW A FAITH-BASED ACTION, LIKE FORGIVENESS OR HELPING, IN FRONT OF CHILDREN.	PRAY FOR WISDOM IN A SPECIFIC PARENTING AREA OF UNCERTAINTY.	WRITE DOWN THREE JOYFUL MOMENTS TO SHARE AT DINNER.
WAKE UP 15 MINUTES EARLY FOR QUIET PRAYER OR MEDITATION.	WRITE DOWN TWO SPIRITUAL GOALS FOR THE NEXT MONTH.